Leadership Lessons

Restaurant Guide

By Andy Griffith

LEGAL DISCLIMAER:

All Rights Reserved. Printed in the United States of America. No part of this publication may be used, reproduced, distributed, or transmitted in any form or by any means, or stored in a database retrieval system without the prior written permission of the Author Andy Griffith. Any unauthorized copying, translating, duplicating, importation or distribution, in whole or in part, by any means, including electronic copying, storage or transmission, is a violation of applicable laws. You do not have resell rights or giveaway rights to any portion of this publication. Only customers that have purchased this publication are authorized to view it. This publication contains material protected under International and Federal Copyright Laws and Treaties. Violations of this copyright will be enforced to the full extent of the law. Brief quotations with full credit to the author of this book embodied in critical articles, social media posts or reviews will be allowed.

For information contact:
www.AndyGriffith.co
Book Cover and Design by Andy Griffith
ISBN 13: 9781093963199

First Edition: August 2018
Copyright © 2018
by Andy Griffith

www.FoodserviceSecrets.com

Dedicated to my mother Karri Griffith.

Thank you for all your wisdom, ethics, and lessons taught to me over my childhood and young adult years.

I wish you were still here to see this...

I Love You.

www.FoodserviceSecrets.com

Table of Contents

INTRODUCTION 1

CHAPTER ONE 7
    THERE TO SOLVE PROBLEMS...

CHAPTER TWO 11
    OWNING THE MISTAKES...

CHAPTER THREE 19
    MESSENGER NOT THE MESSAGE...

CHAPTER FOUR 25
    SKIP THE PROBLEMS OFFER SOLUTIONS...

CHAPTER FIVE 31
    CARE ENOUGH TO ASK...

CHAPTER SIX 39
    STRAIGHT TALK...

CHAPTER SEVEN 49
    ABOVE NOTHING...

CHAPTER EIGHT 55
    BE A GLASS HOUSE...

CONCLUSION 63

ABOUT THE AUTHOR 66

www.FoodserviceSecrets.com

www.FoodserviceSecrets.com

Introduction

As an owner or manager of a hospitality location you can attest to the fact that aside from serving delicious meals in a great environment, the leadership roles played go a long way in ensuring that the business thrives.

A leader plays a significant role in any organization. However, a leader cannot be effective without people that follow them. The art of leadership is the process through which a person leads, direct and influences the affairs of others. A leader is said to be successful when they can maximize the uniqueness of each member of their team.

As a leader in the hospitality industry your guiding people that are the direct link to the source of revenue for the restaurant; the guests. Your leadership goal should be to create a culture within the business that even when you aren't at the store the business still flourishes.

I want you to forget about leadership as a bossy position. This is the most misguided concept of leadership that still effects organizations to date. Yes, leadership does afford you the opportunity of being the boss, but beyond that, it provides a platform for you to make a meaningful impact on the organization's team members.

This guide is going to help transform your thinking by providing strategic concept steps towards building a solid foundation of leadership that is worthy of emulation.

In this guide, you will learn key aspects to become a leader who can take his or her restaurant staff to the next level of increased productivity and engagement. There is so much more to leadership other than having the name tag "Manager" across your shirt. The quality of leadership you dish out will determine the extent to which your team will follow you and the success your business actually has.

You will learn some of the best ways through which you can work with your team to succeed together. Sit tight and enjoy the ride, because this material is loaded with lots of exciting tactics (that I personally use) to help motivate your team to follow your directions.

Now you may wonder why I chose to make a guide about restaurant leadership? The response to that question lies in the fact that the success of any restaurant or business rests on the extent of influence the leader has over their staff. As you read on, several ideas on leadership will be exposed to you that are based on my real-world experiences. I want to you to fully grasp the connection between great leadership skills and the success of your hospitality business.

I urge you to take each sentence seriously and all advice offered. It will help you build a solid team and work environment culture of success. The essence of this guide is to show you why you need to enhance your leadership skills; how you can go about such a transition in your business; and why these lessons are essential to your success. Are you ready to begin the journey? If so, turn the page and let's do this!

Chapter One
There to solve problems...

As much as I hate to say it, as a leader we are there because things don't go right. If everyone showed up on time when scheduled; made all the food correctly and in a timely manner; wore the correct uniforms for their shift; was polite and never made a customer feel put off by attitude; and nothing ever broke down in the store; the list goes on... we wouldn't be needed.

It's because these things don't go perfect that we a called to action. <u>Our role is to solve problems, not become one.</u> I know it can be frustrating to deal with some of these issues on a repeated basis, but once you understand that this is one of the reasons you are there the weight begins to lift.

Instead of getting upset because something goes wrong it's now an expected outcome. I mean hey, we are in a leadership position to solve problems. So why are we surprised, caught off guard, and upset when they happen now that we know this?

The team will come to you to fix things. Don't make it a burden for them to tell you about an issue. Be the hero and solve those issues for your team. This gains trust with them to depend on you for help. Otherwise the staff will be taught, based on your negative responses, to not always inform you of stuff you probably want to know about. I would like to believe as the leader you would like to know if something is wrong... right?

Keep this mindset moving forward so you can be proactive about issues rather then reactive. This will boost trust and moral for your team. As the leader you are there to solve the problems. Plain and simple.

Chapter Two
Owning the mistakes...

Now that we learned that we are there to solve problems lets talk about owning mistakes within the business. When something goes wrong do you blame the person, or do you take ownership of it?

Where I am going with this is that as the leader we need to take full responsibility for how the team performs. This is also another hard subject to swallow for most people. Often, it's much easier to point at others as to why this or that, did or did not happen.

But let's look at it from this angle for just a second. Those of us in leadership probably hired the person. So, we choose to have them on the team. We probably trained the person or had them trained by someone we picked to be their trainer. We also scheduled them to work that shift. So how do we blame them for the mistake? We choose to hire, how to train and where to place them.

It is our responsibilities as leaders to own the problems being made. We have to take an honest look at the scenarios and ask what we should, or could we have done differently. I am not saying we can avoid mistakes, but I am saying we shouldn't blame the person for what happen.

Once you blame someone else for problems you actually loose the power and authority over the problem. If we take ownership of the issues we now have control on how we can fix them from happening again or at least take steps to prevent a repeat situation.

You would be amazed at how much credit and support your team will have for you when you take the blame for something that went wrong. Just imagine you had a rough shift, but you made it to the end. The staff is edgy, and things have been tense, but instead of yelling at others for what they did wrong you pointed out ways you could have made the night better and apologized to them for having to go through it.

You tell the cooks you should have not had the new guy on so soon for a Friday night, but let that new guy know you needed to give him a few more training shifts and its okay, that you admired how hard he tried to keep up and that you appreciate him.

You tell the servers you should have had an extra runner or busser on and it would have helped make the service and table turns faster. You feel bad because it might have affected tips and you care about them making as much money as they can.

Then you tell everyone you will learn from this and do a better job next time. Let that sink in for minute...

Most of your team will be blown away at how humble you are. You will see them tell you it's okay and they start to support you because you took the blame for the mistakes that they already know they made.

You will begin to see much better performance in the long run with this approach verses at the end of a rough shift you are yelling at everyone and pointing out their faults and weaknesses. That type of approach only builds more tension, destroys your moral and cripples your culture.

Moving forward as a leader start owning the mistakes within your business and let the team know you have their backs when things get rough. When you believe in people it's amazing what they will deliver back to you. They will perform better and try harder to hit the potential you see in them.

17

Chapter Three
Messenger not the message...

Early on in my career I made this HUGE mistake. I see a lot of newer managers repeat this leadership foul as well. Just because you have a title it doesn't make you a leader. On the flip side, not all leaders actually have a title either.

People with authority can make the mistake of trying to be the message instead of the messenger. To break this down, they don't explain the why or purpose behind things. They have this idea in their head that I am the boss, leader, owner etc... I don't have to explain myself.

And you know what? Your right, you absolutely don't. But, over time that type of leadership style breeds resentment and a lot of misunderstanding. No one wants to here "That's just how we do it" or "I don't have to explain myself to you" or "Just do what I say". Looking back over your very own life did any of those types of responses breed a desire to follow that person? They didn't, don't and won't. They are off putting and cause you to not be fully engaged.

You might have done what was asked at that time, but it wasn't to the best of your ability and it caused you to say "whatever (insert bad words here)" in your head.

The goal of this guide is to use *Leadership Lessons* to help improve your locations culture and staff moral which in turns grows the performance results of the company.

By being the messenger instead of the message, those same comments come across like this: "The reason we do it this way is because..." or "I apologise, maybe I didn't explain this well, the reason we are doing this is..." or "I need your help and am depending on you because I trust you to handle..."

Each one of those statements said in the tone as the messenger (explaining why's / purposes) verses trying to be the message (commanding orders) goes over much better and is well received. When someone understands the why or purpose behind what they are doing or being asked their buy in rate goes through the roof.

This is a different era than the past. This book is not titled *Command Captain* it is called *Leadership Lessons*. In order to lead you need people willing to follow. In order to lead well they have to respect and trust you, not fear and hate you.

Chapter Four
Skip the problems offer solutions

The title of the chapter isn't to encourage you not to face problems. It's taking it a step further. It's much too easy to walk into a place and point out what's wrong. Anyone can do that, in any business, anywhere.

The real magic and skill is being able to offer solutions. That takes talent. As a leader one of your roles much like we talked about in chapter one is to solve problems. This one focuses on why it's important to offer solutions as a way to build your team up.

Instead of telling your team what they are doing wrong explain to them how to do the task right. Did you get that last sentence? Let's go over it again... Instead of telling your team what they are doing wrong, explain to them how to do the task right. This is a completely different way to address issues.

You can start with asking them why they are doing something a certain way. That might open up a door to ideas you haven't considered. Is there a reason they are doing xyz? You can then lead into to the "why" and "purpose" of doing the tasks the way you want them done.

Often times a person is trying to do what they think is helpful or right. Deep down inside we all want to be winners. No one looks in the mirror and goes I hope I suck today. So, when approaching things that are not being done correctly offer solutions with the purpose and why after you hear them out on why they are doing what they did.

This approach allows your staff to be heard while laying the foundation for a positive coachable moment. No one likes to hear "you're doing that wrong". How much better would it sound when said this way. "Is there a reason you're doing (____) that way...? (they answer) Gotcha... well the reason we want it done this way instead is because (____) ...

moving forward I need your help to make sure we follow that process, cool?"

BOOM! You now respected and heard them. Explained your why and asked them to help you. This is how you build people up, boost moral and drive culture. Remember, it's not the problem that's the issue, it's how we respond and provide solutions that make all the difference.

Chapter Five
Care enough to ask...

Being a leader in hospitality comes with a lot of moving parts. Often it feels like there is a 1,000+ things to do each day. Trust me I get it. What happens though because of this is us leaders often miss a very key element to building culture.

We forget to ask our team members how they're doing, and I mean really asking them. Without prying, ask how their family is, how is school going, what are there hobbies and how are those going... your team will share with you what they feel comfortable sharing. You can also always say to them that you are not trying to pry, and they don't need to share anything they are uncomfortable with. This practice simply lets them know you care about who they are as a person.

I am not saying nor suggesting you become best friends with your team. It is suggested and healthy to keep some clear lines, but you should take an interest in them as individuals. They could have hobbies and interest unknown to you. Once you take time to get to know them better you can find ways to help them achieve results towards those outside work activities.

Often in hospitality the staff has a second job or is going to school. Say you learn person X studies theatre. You know one of your regulars works at a local show place. It doesn't hurt to introduce them. Don't be scared about them "leaving" you. They will leave one way or the other if that truly is their passion. Wouldn't you rather be someone who helped a person reach their goals then someone who tried to hold them back?

We can all look back on our lives and remember the ones who cared and who helped us out. By taking time to care you're going to make a real impact with your staff. They will in return care about your goals with the business. They will have your back when you get shorthanded. They will refer friends to come work for you and rave about how awesome it is being a part of the team.

If you take sleep out of the equation some people spend more time at work, then at home. Especially if they have 2 jobs or go to school. Work is where they have their friendships and it takes up most of their lives. It only takes a few questions a day to make your business more meaningful to your team. Don't get me wrong we are all there to do a job, but work can be a fun place that people actually enjoy being at.

It's those sayings you hear. *"People don't care how much you know. They want to know how much you* care." Or, *"people don't quit a job, they quit a leader."*

Having a leader who takes time to teach you constructively how to do tasks, takes the blame when things go wrong, and cares about who you are as a person is the leader people will follow.

Don't forget to ask your team what their career and life goals are. You may find that there are ways to build someone up within your location to know multiple roles and be a growing asset to the business. That dish person may want to learn how to cook. The hostess may want to serve. The server may want to bartend, and all of them may want to be a manager one day.

The real quality of leadership is how you empower others to become better and hit their goals. It doesn't mean you give them everything they want right when they want it. It does mean however that you lay out a clear game plan with them to help them hit those milestone achievements along the way.

Take the time to care enough to ask. Be a leader and a shield. Lead them towards success and shield them from hurdles along the way.

Chapter Six
Straight talk...

Through most of this guide we have went deep on how to approach situations to build people up and how to create a culture of ownership where people want to follow you. This chapter is for those on your team who may not be "getting" it.

Some of you may have been reading all this thinking yeah, it all sounds good, makes sense, but I have team members who will exploit this, take advantage of that, or just won't jump on board. You may have already been implementing these tactics, but you have someone who just won't get with the program. Well this is the chapter you have been waiting for.

Straight talk is what it is. Straight. Talk. Part of being a leader will entail having those difficult conversations from time to time.

As a leader it's important you position yourself as an authority figure. By no means in the earlier chapters do I expect you to take insubordination from those you lead. In fact, embrace it dead on, and be quick to discuss issues. Just be sure to do so with class.

Always criticize in private and praise in public. Should you have a problem with a team member or they speak out of line. Ask them to follow you so you can finish this conversation in private. Address their attitude dead on and explain your goal and role (as the messenger) and ask them why they are acting the way they do.

We are not telling them what they need to do here... We want to address the situation with an "I / feel" sentence.

Here's what that is; "I feel (___be open here) when a person (don't say their name) does X (whatever they are doing). It makes me think (___) about them. I respect you and what to understand you better. What's causing this X (what they did) to happen? You will find that when you take the time to understand someone and use the "I / feel" statement it lowers tension and opens up straight talk. It's hard to argue with you about how you feel about a situation and by putting it in the 3rd person you are generalizing to the issue instead of confronting the person.

Then explain that as the leader there is a "certain level of respect that is needed from all team members. if they understand that and are they able to do so?" 90% of the time they will say yes. The 10% that don't please see next couple paragraphs. Then end with "can WE move past the scenario to work better TOGETHER as team?"

Granted if they won't see that you are trying to diffuse a heated situation and keep pushing you or will not work to resolve the addressed issue then you have to move towards actions that may include suspension and, or termination.

That conversation could be similar to "Hey (name), I need to speak with you for a moment." Take them somewhere private. "Listen we both talked about X, but I am still not seeing a change... Please understand I feel X when a person does X. It makes me think X. After we both talked, and X has continued to happen it leaves me no choice but to X. I hope you are able to understand?"

You don't have to say these words for word. The goal of the leader is to remain calm and not add any gas to the problem. Remember we are solving problems. The "I / feel" statement makes it much less confronting than doing a "Why are you... or You did this... or Your doing this...", it puts the scenario in to a 3rd person realm which helps both party's step back for a moment.

Another aspect of straight talk but is also the flip side of owning mistakes is to praise in public. As the leader, fall on the sword for the team but give them the lime light when things go good. Always point to someone else when being recognized. You see it in awards speeches all the time. "I want to thank God, my family, my coaches, etc..."

Try to find ways to edify or praise your staff in public as often as possible. Celebrate wins left and right. Tell your cooks how awesome a dish looks; commend your bartender for slinging drinks out like no other; praise your server for how great they are at interacting with customers; thank you bussers and dish for being the back bone of everything working since you have clean tables and plates to serve; honour your hosts for handling the crowd of people at the font with poise and grace.

How often does your team hear "good job" from you? Think back to when you were not in leadership. When your leader told you about something great you did I bet you later went home and told your family and friends. As I said earlier it's easy to spot problems, be a master at spotting what's working.

The key aspect behind straight talk is to be genuine and care enough to have the conversations both good and bad. Just be sure to always do it with respect and in return your staff will respect you back.

Even with the ones you may end up having to let go, continue to treat them with respect. Multiple times using these techniques I have had a good handshake and an apology from them after we had to part ways.

Chapter Seven
Above nothing...

You have probably heard the term servant leadership. This is very similar to that concept. As the leader don't start to count yourself above doing things. In fact, when you do those odd jobs no one likes to do it bonds you and your staff together.

This doesn't mean you should do everyone's job for them. They are there for a reason. However, what if you cleaned the mess made in the bathrooms for your busser everyone once and while. Think they would appreciate you and be more than willing to help you when you really needed something?

What if you had to take a table or two just to get over the hump in the shift, but then you gave the tips to split with the other servers (legally you may have to). Think they wouldn't be impressed?

What if you are short a food runner so you work expo that night helping keep the server's tables in check. How about your down a cook and there is no other option but to be on the grill with your team? Think your chefs would respect you more. It might even create some fun because they can smoke you on the line, but hey you are there to help and care enough to drown with them rather than watch from the side lines as they crash and burn.

For the record, try your best to stay in role that allows you to see the floor, but this is not always going to be the case. Just remember, you're mission is to never be above whatever is needed to get the job done. It wont always be the ideal shift ran, but when your team sees you are not above working beside them with a positive mental attitude they are more inclined to strive for excellence alongside you.

When you do get put in those scenarios I want to strive the phrase <u>positive mental attitude</u>. You are the thermostat and the team is the thermometer. You set the degree, pace, and ambiance. They will rise or fall to it.

Once the leader loses it, the rest of the team follows quickly. If the leader is on point mentally, even when it's not going well, it helps keep everyone else from crumbling. Coach your team through each shift. Remember all great shifts are managed, they don't just happen by mistake. Be hands on and proactive to do what's needed, when it's needed.

Chapter Eight
Be a glass house…

I am not a fan of secrets. This guide is sharing with you my tactics used to operate multimillion-dollar stores, oversee teams of 70 people and advise 100 plus locations. You are getting to glean these tips and tricks from my 17 plus years' experience of working in the industry from a kitchen help to a chef; to general manager and multi-unit gm; to a hospitality business advisor.

This is not a praise me type moment. It's a you're getting first hand access to proven methods that work moment, based on actual use in the field. One thing I have learned is the more transparent I am, the more success I have.

How that applies to you as a leader is by sharing more information verses less with your team, you will actually help them better understand why certain choices are being made over others.

I'm not sure of your comfort level, but you would be amazed by how much money your staff thinks the business is making. Ask them sometime how much out of each dollar generated do they think is profit. The answers will shock you. Ask them if they realize you have to match their taxes on payroll checks. I bet they will say that's crazy.

There is a movement happening called open book management. The concept is to start sharing business financial with your team. When they see how much you spend on food each week, grazing and comps make more sense as to why they hurt the company. When they see how much you spend in payroll (total sum not each person's pay rate / check) they start to understand why you make cuts when it is slow.

By sharing more information rather than little to none they get equipped to be able to help you improve areas of your business. They understand what the big goals are and how they can each make their own impact. All of the other chapters focused on being a leader that has a following and a company culture that people want to be apart of. By tying in this element here, you now have a group thinking about ways to help improve the business.

When they learn that since the new place down the street opened or the slow season hits sales drop by X, this means we have to adjust labor. It's not viewed as you are just taking hours away from everyone.

You can set up milestones of if we hit X then everyone gets a prize. Make it fun and track progress weekly to update on a scoreboard. You could also have nightly goals of who ever sells X gets Y. The idea is to think of ways to use everyone talents for different parts of the business. Chef's hit X food cost they get Y. Bartenders get X liquor costs they get Y. Total sales get X servers get Y. Starting to get the idea?

Another concept for everyone to realize is the busier you are the less jobs you do. What I mean is, if it's slow you may have a salad person who also fries appetizers. If you were busy enough with demand you could have 1 fry person and 1 salad person. Hence, the busier you are the less jobs you do.

This chapter also ties back to being the messenger. Sharing business performance information and being open about why choices are made makes you a glass house. Your staff will trust you more and understand the purpose of why.

Don't make the mistake of thinking if I teach this person something they will take my job or screw me over. Yes, you need to be selective on what you feel comfortable sharing and with whom, but the goal is to empower others. The more people know the better they can help affect the results.

Conclusion

This is the special message I have for you; be deliberate about implementing all you have learned. You've now become a leader for life and a mentor to those on your team. Even after you leave an organization the leadership qualities you learned and taught don't fade away. Often, it's how an organization perfroms after you leave that says a lot about your legacy as a leader. Keep the fire burning and continue to improve on all that you've learned.

Your team will be grateful for these new approaches. Your customers will be happier as a result of the improved culture within your business, and your company will thrive because of it. More importantly, you will be excited about going to work because you know it is no longer about work now, but about how you impact the lives of those you lead.

Thank you for reading, I hope you are now ready to disrupt your leadership patterns with these lessons.

As a manager or owner of the business, so much is expected of you. With these lessons you can surpass all those expectations and more. There are no limitations for you or what you can accomplish through your team. Tackle it day by day.

GET AFTER IT!

- *Andy Griffith*

@iamandygriffith

About The Author

Andy Griffith is a 18-year veteran of the Hospitality Industry. He started as a kitchen help and has since worked his way up holding positions of hibachi chef, sushi chef, general manager, multi-unit manager and business advisor. He lives in Oklahoma City, OK with his darling wife Ruth.

When he is not helping others succeed in the foodservice sector, he enjoys playing online games, reading personal development books, physical fitness activities and watching action, drama, and sci-fi movies.

@IamAndyGriffith

Facebook | Instagram | Twitter | LinkedIn

www.AndyGriffith.co

www.FoodserviceSecrets.com

www.ingramcontent.com/pod-product-compliance
Lightning Source LLC
Chambersburg PA
CBHW072205170526
45158CB00004BB/1771